*mini*atlas of Millennium Development Goals

BUILDING A BETTER WORLD

THE WORLD BANK
Washington, D.C.

Copyright © 2005
The International Bank for
Reconstruction and Development /
The World Bank
1818 H Street, NW
Washington, DC 20433
Telephone 202-473-1000
Internet www.worldbank.org
E-mail feedback@worldbank.org

ISBN: 0-8213-6175-9   978-0-8213-6175-7
e-ISBN: 0-8213-6176-7

Published for the World Bank by
Myriad Editions Limited
6–7 Old Steine, Brighton BN1 3EJ, UK
www.MyriadEditions.com

Printed and bound in Hong Kong

Library of Congress cataloging-in-publication data has been
applied for.

Other Titles in the *mini*atlas Series

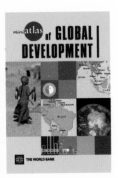

miniAtlas of Global Development
An at-a-glance guide to the most pressing development issues facing the world today. Highlights key social, economic, and environmental data for 208 of the world's economies.
ISBN: 0-8213-5596-1

Green miniAtlas
A snapshot, presented in maps and charts, of the world's most urgent environmental challenges: increasing pollution, the rising demand for energy and food, declining biodiversity, and the pressure on water resources.
ISBN: 0-8213-5870-7

Available at better bookstores
To order go to **www.worldbank.org/publications**
or email: books@worldbank.org

Goal 8 Develop a global partnership for development

- Develop further an open, rule-based, predictable, nondiscriminatory trading and financial system (includes a commitment to good governance, development, and poverty reduction – both nationally and internationally)
- Address the special needs of the least developed countries (includes tariff- and quota-free access for exports, enhanced program of debt relief for and cancellation of official bilateral debt, and more generous ODA for countries committed to poverty reduction)
- Address the special needs of landlocked countries and small island developing states (through the Program of Action for the Sustainable Development of Small Island Developing States and 22nd General Assembly provisions)

- Deal comprehensively with the debt problems of developing countries through national and international measures in order to make debt sustainable in the long term
- In cooperation with developing countries, develop and implement strategies for decent and productive work for youth
- In cooperation with pharmaceutical companies, provide access to affordable essential drugs in developing countries
- In cooperation with the private sector, make available the benefits of new technologies, especially information and communications technologies

D0368541

Contents

Preface

The Millennium Development Goals are a challenge the global community has set for itself. They are a challenge to poor countries to demonstrate good governance and a commitment to poverty reduction. And they are a challenge to wealthy countries to make good on their promise to support economic and social development. The Millennium Development Goals have captured the world's attention, in part because they can be measured, as this little book demonstrates. More important, the goals address our most human concerns for the welfare of everyone with whom we share this planet.

We are now one third of the way to the target date of 2015, and there are 100 million fewer people living in extreme poverty than in 1990. By 2015, 500 million more will have achieved at least a minimally acceptable standard of living – the greatest decrease in poverty since the beginning of the industrial revolution. But progress has been uneven, and many of the poorest countries, especially in Africa, lag behind.

Extreme poverty means having less than $1 to meet your daily needs. But poverty is not measured in money alone. Poor people lack education, they lack health care, and they often live on wasted lands or in city slums. Solving these problems will require a substantial investment in people as well as in physical assets. Wealthy countries can help, not only through their aid programs – which are important – but also by opening their markets and by sharing knowledge. Most important of all, developing countries must unleash the potential of their citizens, empowering them to create a place for themselves and their children in the world.

François Bourguignon
Senior Vice President and Chief Economist
The World Bank Group

THE WORLD BY REGION

Low- and middle-income economies

- East Asia and Pacific
- Eastern Europe and Central Asia
- Latin America and Caribbean
- Middle East and North Africa
- South Asia
- Sub-Saharan Africa

High-income economies

- OECD
- other
- no data

Iceland
Faeroe Is. (Den)
Norway
Finland
Sweden
Estonia
Latvia
United Kingdom
Denmark
Lithuania
Ireland
Isle of Man (UK)
Russian Fed.
Neth.
Poland
Belarus
Channel Is. (UK)
Belgium
Germany
Luxembourg
Liecht.
Czech Rep.
Slovak Rep.
France
Switz.
Austria
Hungary
Romania
Slovenia
Serb. and Montenegro
Andorra
Monaco
Croatia
Bos. and Herz.
Bulgaria
S. Marino
Portugal
Spain
Vatican City
Italy
Albania
F.Y.R. Macedonia
Gibraltar (UK)
Tunisia
Malta
Greece

Canada

United States

Bermuda (UK)

Mexico
Cuba
Puerto Rico (US)
Virgin Is. (US)
Antigua and Barbuda
Cayman Is. (UK)
Dominican Rep.
St. Kitts & Nevis
Guadeloupe (Fr)
Dominica
Guatemala
Belize
Jamaica
Haiti
Martinique (Fr)
St. Vincent and the Grenadines
El Salvador
Honduras
Antilles (Neth)
St. Lucia
Barbados
Nicaragua
Aruba (Neth)
Grenada
Trinidad and Tobago
Costa Rica
R. B. de Venezuela
Guyana
Panama
Colombia
Suriname
French Guiana (Fr)

Ecuador
Peru
Brazil

Bolivia
Paraguay
Chile
Uruguay
Argentina

Morocco
Former Spanish Sahara
Algeria
Libya
Cape Verde
Mauritania
Mali
Niger
Chad
The Gambia
Senegal
Burkina Faso
Nigeria
Guinea-Bissau
Guinea
Côte d'Ivoire
Ghana
Togo
Benin
Central African Rep.
Sierra Leone
Liberia
Equatorial Guinea
Cameroon
Gabon
São Tomé and Principe
Rep. Congo
Dem. Rep. of Congo
Angola
Namibia
Botswana
South Africa

6

The World by Region

The World Bank's main criterion for classifying economies is gross national income (GNI) per capita. Every economy is classified as low income, middle income, or high income. Low-income economies are those with a GNI per capita of $765 or less in 2003. Middle-income economies are those with a GNI per capita of more than $765 but less than $9,386. High-income economies are those with a GNI per capita of $9,386 or more. Low- and middle-income economies are sometimes referred to as developing economies.

Geographic regions used in this atlas include only low- and middle-income economies

Eradicating Poverty and Hunger

The Millennium Development Goals call for a reduction in the proportion of people living on less than $1 a day to half the 1990 level by 2015. There has been remarkable progress. Since 1990 extreme poverty in developing countries has fallen from 28 percent to 21 percent in 2001.

If current projections of economic growth are met, global poverty will fall to 10 percent by 2015. And while poverty would not be eradicated, that would bring us much closer to the day when we can say that all the world's people have at least the bare minimum to meet their daily needs.

The Goals also call for a halving of the proportion of people who suffer from hunger between 1990 and 2015. Hunger and malnutrition often go with poverty, but even where poverty rates are falling, hundreds of millions of people do not obtain enough food to meet their daily needs, and millions more children are malnourished. Poverty and hunger will remain wherever poor health and lack of education deprive people of productive employment; environmental resources have been depleted or spoiled; and corruption, conflict, and misgovernance waste public resources and discourage private investment.

Child malnutrition
This is not only the result of poor diet, but of disease, lack of care, and poverty.

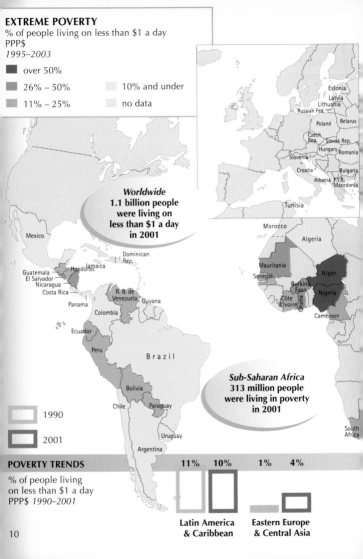

EXTREME POVERTY

% of people living on less than $1 a day
PPP$

1995–2003

- over 50%
- 26% – 50%
- 11% – 25%
- 10% and under
- no data

Worldwide
1.1 billion people were living on less than $1 a day in 2001

Sub-Saharan Africa
313 million people were living in poverty in 2001

Estonia
Latvia
Lithuania
Russian Fed.
Poland
Belarus
Czech Rep.
Slovak Rep.
Slovenia
Hungary
Romania
Croatia
Bulgaria
Albania
F.Y.R. Macedonia
Tunisia

Morocco
Algeria
Mauritania
Senegal
Niger
Burkina Faso
Nigeria
Ghana
Côte d'Ivoire
Cameroon
South Africa

Mexico
Dominican Rep.
Jamaica
Guatemala
Honduras
El Salvador
Nicaragua
Costa Rica
Panama
R. B. de Venezuela
Guyana
Colombia
Ecuador
Peru
Brazil
Bolivia
Paraguay
Chile
Uruguay
Argentina

1990
2001

POVERTY TRENDS

% of people living on less than $1 a day
PPP$ *1990–2001*

11%	10%	1%	4%
Latin America & Caribbean		Eastern Europe & Central Asia	

10

Poverty

The percentage of people living in extreme poverty has fallen fastest in Asia, notably in China and India. In the rest of the developing world, poverty rates have increased or fallen only slightly.

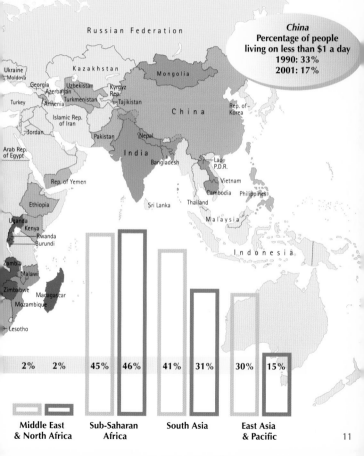

China
Percentage of people living on less than $1 a day
1990: 33%
2001: 17%

2%	2%	45%	46%	41%	31%	30%	15%

Middle East & North Africa · **Sub-Saharan Africa** · **South Asia** · **East Asia & Pacific**

MALNOURISHED CHILDREN

% of children under five years
who are malnourished
1995–2003

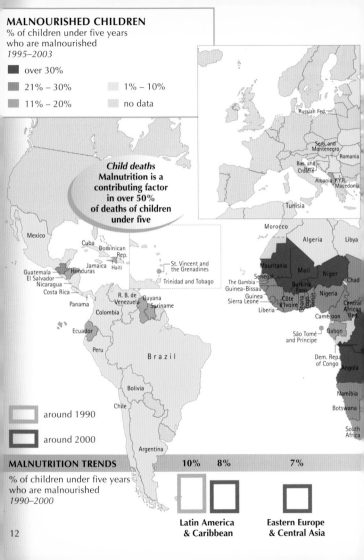

- over 30%
- 21% – 30%
- 11% – 20%
- 1% – 10%
- no data

Child deaths
**Malnutrition is a
contributing factor
in over 50%
of deaths of children
under five**

Russian Fed.

Serb. and
Montenegro
Romania
Bos. and
Croatia
Albania F.Y.R.
Macedonia

Tunisia

Mexico

Cuba
Dominican
Rep.
Jamaica Haiti
Guatemala Honduras
El Salvador
Nicaragua
Costa Rica
Panama

St. Vincent and
the Grenadines

Trinidad and Tobago

R. B. de
Venezuela Guyana
Colombia Suriname

Ecuador

Peru

B r a z i l

Bolivia

Chile

Argentina

Morocco

Algeria Libya

Mauritania Mali Niger Chad
Senegal Burkina
The Gambia Faso Nigeria
Guinea-Bissau Guinea Benin Central
Sierra Leone Côte Togo African
d'Ivoire Ghana Rep.
Liberia Cameroon

São Tomé Gabon
and Principe

Dem. Rep.
of Congo Angola

Namibia

Botswana

South
Africa

around 1990

around 2000

MALNUTRITION TRENDS

% of children under five years
who are malnourished
1990–2000

10%   8%

7%

**Latin America
& Caribbean**

**Eastern Europe
& Central Asia**

12

Malnutrition

Malnutrition rates among children under five years of age in the developing world fell from 47 percent in 1970 to 27 percent in 2000. Even so, 150 million children in low- and middle-income economies are still malnourished.

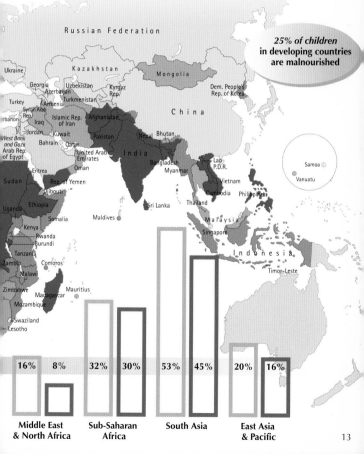

25% of children in developing countries are malnourished

16%	8%	32%	30%	53%	45%	20%	16%
Middle East & North Africa		**Sub-Saharan Africa**		**South Asia**		**East Asia & Pacific**	

Goal 2

Achieving Universal Primary Education

Education is the foundation of democratic societies and globally competitive economies. It is the basis for reducing poverty and inequality, improving health, enabling the use of new technologies, and creating and spreading knowledge. In an increasingly complex, knowledge-dependent world, primary education, as the gateway to higher levels of education, must be the first priority.

Since 1990 the countries of the world have called for all children to be able to complete primary school, but more than 100 million children of primary-school age remain out of school, most of them in South Asia and Sub-Saharan Africa, and the majority of them are girls. To reach the Millennium Development Goals by 2015, school systems with low completion rates will need to start now to train teachers, build classrooms, and improve the quality of education. They will also have to remove barriers to attendance, such as fees and lack of transportation, and address parents' concern for the safety of their children.

Universal enrollment
50 developing countries had met the goal by 2003;
7 were on track to meet the goal by 2015;
58 risk missing the goal;
39 lack adequate data to monitor progress.

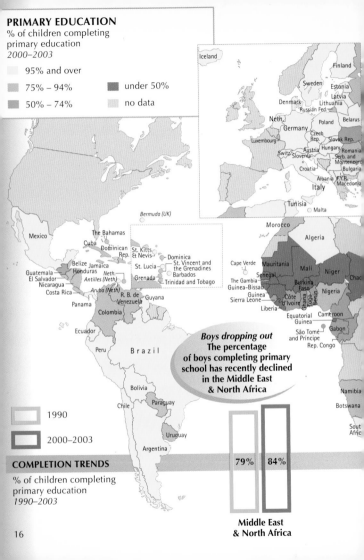

PRIMARY EDUCATION

% of children completing
primary education
2000–2003

- 95% and over
- 75% – 94%
- 50% – 74%
- under 50%
- no data

Boys dropping out
**The percentage
of boys completing primary
school has recently declined
in the Middle East
& North Africa**

1990

2000–2003

COMPLETION TRENDS

% of children completing
primary education
1990–2003

79%   84%

**Middle East
& North Africa**

Iceland
Finland
Sweden
Estonia
Denmark   Latvia
Lithuania
Russian Fed.
Neth.   Poland   Belarus
Germany
Luxembourg   Czech
Rep.   Slovak Rep.
Switz.   Austria Hungary   Romania
Slovenia   Serb. and
Croatia   Montenegro
Bulgaria
Albania   F.Y.R.
Macedonia
Italy

Tunisia   Malta

Bermuda (UK)

Mexico
The Bahamas
Cuba
Dominican
Belize   Jamaica   Rep.   St. Kitts
& Nevis   Dominica
Guatemala   Neth.   St. Lucia   St. Vincent and
El Salvador   Antilles (Neth)   the Grenadines
Honduras   Grenada   Barbados
Nicaragua   Trinidad and Tobago
Costa Rica   Aruba (Neth)
Panama   R. B. de   Guyana
Venezuela
Colombia
Ecuador

Peru   B r a z i l

Bolivia

Chile   Paraguay

Uruguay

Argentina

Morocco
Algeria
Cape Verde   Mauritania   Mali   Niger   Chad
Senegal   Burkina
The Gambia   Faso   Nigeria
Guinea-Bissau   Guinea
Sierra Leone   Côte
d'Ivoire   Cameroon
Liberia   Equatorial   São Tomé
Guinea   and Principe   Gabon
Rep. Congo

Namibia

Botswana

Sout
Afric

16

School Attendance

In many areas of the world more than 90 percent of all children complete primary school. In the Middle East, Africa, and South Asia, rates are lower but have improved since 1990.

Girls lose out
Fewer than 50% of girls in Africa complete primary school

50%	59%		74%	80%
Sub-Saharan Africa			South Asia	

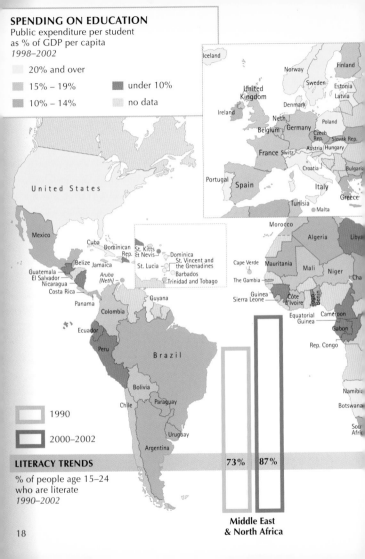

SPENDING ON EDUCATION

Public expenditure per student
as % of GDP per capita
1998–2002

- 20% and over
- 15% – 19%
- 10% – 14%
- under 10%
- no data

LITERACY TRENDS

% of people age 15–24
who are literate
1990–2002

1990

2000–2002

73%   87%

**Middle East
& North Africa**

18

Education Expenditure

To increase enrollment and provide better education, school systems have to invest in training teachers and improving facilities. But many poor countries already spend a substantial share of their GDP on education.

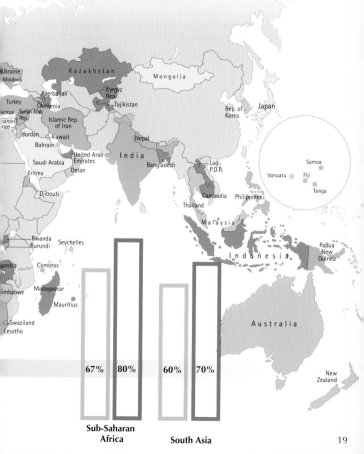

Promoting Gender Equality

Gender inequality starts early and keeps women at a disadvantage throughout their lives. In some countries, infant girls are less likely to survive than infant boys because of parental discrimination and neglect. Girls are more likely to drop out of school and to receive less education than boys because the economic value of their work at home exceeds the perceived value of schooling. But when a country educates both its boys and its girls, economic productivity tends to rise, maternal and infant mortality rates usually fall, fertility rates decline, and the health and education prospects of the next generation improve.

Three regions lag behind in providing girls full access to primary and secondary school: South Asia, Sub-Saharan Africa, and the Middle East and North Africa. But countries with the widest gender gaps have made progress, and renewed efforts to get all children into school will create more opportunities for girls. That is not all that is needed. Empowering women means having an equal voice in all decisions which affect their lives: in the family, in the marketplace, and in government.

Seats in national governments
Only 15% were held by women in 2003, hardly any improvement on the 13% in 1990.

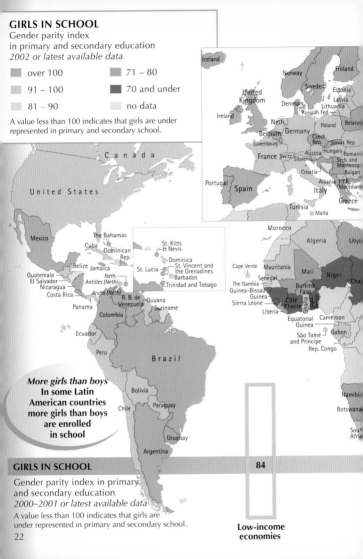

GIRLS IN SCHOOL

Gender parity index
in primary and secondary education
2002 or latest available data

- over 100
- 91 – 100
- 81 – 90
- 71 – 80
- 70 and under
- no data

A value less than 100 indicates that girls are under represented in primary and secondary school.

Iceland

Norway Sweden Finland
Estonia
United Denmark Latvia
Kingdom Lithuania
Russian Fed.
Ireland Neth. Poland Belarus
Belgium Germany
Luxembourg Czech Slovak Rep.
France Switz. Austria Hungary Romania
Slovenia Serb. and
Croatia Montenegro
Portugal Spain Albania F.Y.R. Bulgaria
Italy Macedonia
Greece
Tunisia
Malta

Canada

United States

Mexico
The Bahamas
Cuba
Dominican
Belize Jamaica Rep.
Guatemala *Neth.*
El Salvador *Antilles (Neth.)*
Nicaragua *Aruba (Neth.)*
Costa Rica
Panama R. B. de
Venezuela Guyana
Colombia Suriname

St. Kitts
& Nevis
Dominica
St. Lucia St. Vincent and
the Grenadines
Barbados
Trinidad and Tobago

Morocco Algeria Libya

Cape Verde Mauritania
Senegal Mali Niger Cha
The Gambia Burkina
Guinea-Bissau Faso
Guinea Sierra Leone Côte
d'Ivoire
Liberia

Equatorial Cameroon
Guinea
São Tomé Gabon
and Principe
Rep. Congo

Ecuador

Peru

Brazil

More girls than boys
**In some Latin
American countries
more girls than boys
are enrolled
in school**

Bolivia

Paraguay
Chile

Namibia

Botswana

Uruguay

Sou
Afric

Argentina

GIRLS IN SCHOOL

Gender parity index in primary
and secondary education
2000–2001 or latest available data
A value less than 100 indicates that girls are
under represented in primary and secondary school.

84

Low-income
economies

22

Equality in Education

O ver the past decade, gender difference in school attendance has been greatly reduced, but many girls still do not have equal access to education. The difference is greatest in regions with the lowest overall primary completion rates and the lowest incomes.

Almost equal
Low- and middle-income countries in East Asia and Pacific have almost achieved equal enrollment of boys and girls in school

Middle-income economies: **98**

High-income economies: **101**

WAGE EMPLOYMENT

Women in wage employment
in non-agricultural sector as % of men
2000–2003

- 50% and over
- 40% – 49%
- 30% – 39%
- 20% – 29%
- under 20%
- no data

Europe inset

Iceland

Norway, Sweden, Finland

United Kingdom, Denmark, Estonia, Latvia, Lithuania, Russian Fed.

Ireland, Neth., Belgium, Germany, Poland, Belarus

Luxembourg, Czech Rep., Slovak Rep.

France, Switz., Austria, Hungary, Romania

S. Marino, Slovenia, Serb. and Montenegro, Bulgaria

Andorra, Croatia, F.Y.R. Macedonia

Portugal, Spain, Italy, Albania, Greece

Gibraltar (UK), Tunisia, Malta

Main map labels

Canada

United States

Mexico

Bermuda (UK)

The Bahamas

Cuba

Cayman Is. (UK), Dominican Rep.

Puerto Rico (US)

Belize, Jamaica, Guadeloupe (Fr), Dominica

Guatemala, Honduras, Martinique (Fr), St. Lucia, Barbados

El Salvador, Neth. Antilles (Neth), Grenada, Trinidad and Tobago

Costa Rica, Aruba (Neth)

Panama, R. B. de Venezuela, Suriname, French Guiana (Fr)

Colombia

Ecuador

Peru

Brazil

Bolivia

Paraguay

Chile

Uruguay

Argentina

Morocco, Algeria

Burkina Faso, Côte d'Ivoire

Namibia, Botswana

Latin America and the Caribbean
Women's share of the labor market increased from 39% to 43% between 1990 and 2002

WAGE EMPLOYMENT

Women in wage employment
in non-agricultural sector
as % of men
2000–2003

43% — Latin America & Caribbean

46% — Eastern Europe & Central Asia

Equality in Employment

Wage employment in modern sectors of the economy offers greater security and access to other social and economic benefits. Women typically occupy low-paid, low-status jobs, or work in family enterprises.

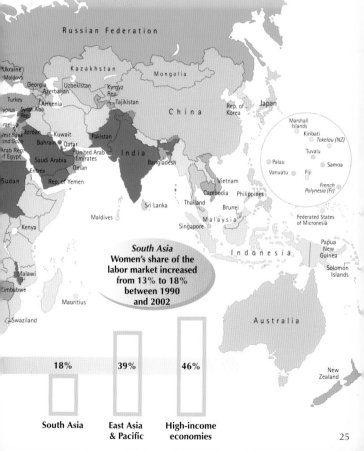

South Asia
Women's share of the labor market increased from 13% to 18% between 1990 and 2002

South Asia	East Asia & Pacific	High-income economies
18%	39%	46%

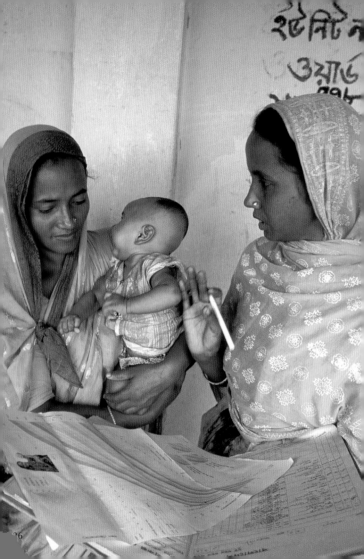

Reducing Child Mortality

Every year almost 11 million children in developing countries die before the age of five, most from causes that are readily preventable in rich countries: acute respiratory infections, diarrhea, measles, and malaria. Rapid improvements before 1990 gave hope that mortality rates for infants and children under five could be cut by two-thirds in the following 25 years.

Progress slowed almost everywhere in the 1990s. Only two regions – Latin America and the Caribbean, and Eastern Europe and Central Asia – may be on track to achieve the target. Progress has been particularly slow in Sub-Saharan Africa, where civil disturbances and the HIV/AIDS epidemic have driven up rates of infant and child deaths. According to the most recent data, only 33 countries are making enough progress to reduce under-five mortality rates to one-third of their 1990 level and save the lives of millions of children. Improvements in water supply, sanitation, and access to health services are needed to make faster progress.

Child mortality
Almost half of all deaths of children under five occur in Sub-Saharan Africa.

CHILD DEATHS

Expected number of deaths of children under five per 1,000 children
2002–2003

- 200 and over
- 150 – 199
- 100 – 149
- 50 – 99
- under 50
- no data

Iceland

Norway Finland

Sweden Estonia

United
Kingdom Denmark Latvia

Russian Fed. Lithuania

Ireland Neth. Germany Poland Belarus

Belgium Czech Ukraine

Luxembourg Liecht. Rep. Slovak Rep.

France Switz. Austria Hungary Romania

Slovenia Serb. and Moldova

S. Marino Croatia Bos. and Bulgaria

Andorra Monaco Herz. Montenegro

Portugal Spain Italy Albania F.Y.R. Macedonia

Greece

Tunisia

Malta

Canada

United States

Mexico

The Bahamas

Cuba Dominican St. Kitts Antigua and Barbuda

Rep. & Nevis

Belize Jamaica Haiti Dominica

Guatemala St. Lucia St. Vincent and

El Salvador Honduras Grenada the Grenadines

Nicaragua Barbados

Costa Rica Trinidad and Tobago

Panama R. B. de Guyana

Venezuela Suriname

Colombia

Ecuador

Peru Brazil

Bolivia

Chile Paraguay

Uruguay

Argentina

Morocco

Algeria Libya

Cape Verde Mauritania Mali Niger Chad

Senegal Burkina

The Gambia Faso Nigeria

Guinea-Bissau Guinea Benin Central

Sierra Leone Côte Ghana Togo African

d'Ivoire Rep.

Liberia Cameroon

Equatorial

Guinea Gabon

São Tomé Rep. Congo

and Príncipe Dem. Rep.

of Congo

Angola

Namibia

Botswana

South

Africa

1990

2003

MORTALITY TRENDS

Expected number of deaths
of children under five
per 1,000 children
1990–2003

	Low-income economies		Middle-income economies	
	149	123	55	37

28

Child Mortality

Mortality rates for children under five in developing countries have dropped by 16 percent since 1990. Yet 30,000 children die each day, most from preventable causes, and almost half of them in Sub-Saharan Africa.

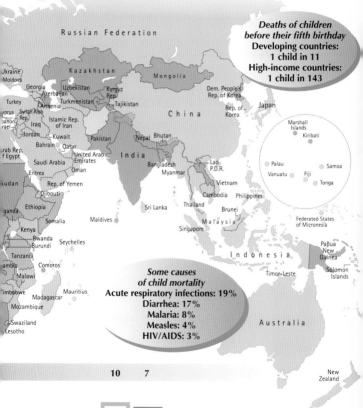

Russian Federation

Ukraine
Moldova
Georgia
Turkey
Cyprus
Lebanon
Israel
Arab Rep.
of Egypt
Sudan
Eritrea
Djibouti
Uganda
Ethiopia
Kenya
Rwanda
Burundi
Tanzania
Zambia
Malawi
Zimbabwe
Mozambique
Swaziland
Lesotho
Comoros
Madagascar
Mauritius
Seychelles
Maldives
Somalia
Rep. of Yemen
Saudi Arabia
Oman
United Arab Emirates
Bahrain
Qatar
Kuwait
Iraq
Jordan
Syrian Arab Rep.
Armenia
Azerbaijan
Islamic Rep. of Iran
Turkmenistan
Uzbekistan
Kazakhstan
Kyrgyz Rep.
Tajikistan
Mongolia
China
Nepal
Bhutan
Pakistan
India
Bangladesh
Myanmar
Sri Lanka
Lao P.D.R.
Thailand
Cambodia
Vietnam
Malaysia
Singapore
Brunei
Philippines
Indonesia
Timor-Leste
Dem. People's Rep. of Korea
Rep. of Korea
Japan
Marshall Islands
Kiribati
Palau
Vanuatu
Fiji
Samoa
Tonga
Federated States of Micronesia
Papua New Guinea
Solomon Islands
Australia
New Zealand

Deaths of children before their fifth birthday
Developing countries:
1 child in 11
High-income countries:
1 child in 143

Some causes of child mortality
Acute respiratory infections: 19%
Diarrhea: 17%
Malaria: 8%
Measles: 4%
HIV/AIDS: 3%

10   7

High-income
economies

29

IMMUNIZATION

% of children under 12 months
immunized against measles
2003

- 90% and over
- 75% – 89%
- 60% – 74%
- under 60%
- no data

IMMUNIZATION TRENDS

% of children under 12 months
immunized against measles
1990–2003

1990
2003

Latin America & Caribbean		Middle East & North Africa	
76%	93%	84%	92%

Immunization

The incidence of measles is on the decline in developing countries. Yet measles continues to strike 30 million children a year, killing more than 600,000, and sometimes resulting in blindness or deafness.

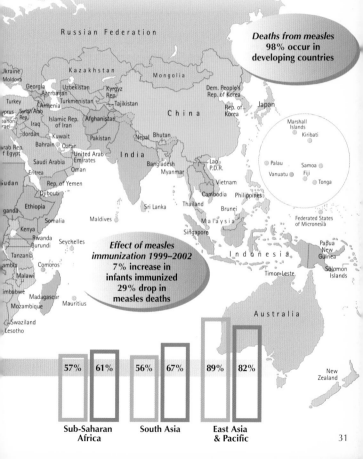

Deaths from measles 98% occur in developing countries

Effect of measles immunization 1999–2002 7% increase in infants immunized 29% drop in measles deaths

Sub-Saharan Africa		South Asia		East Asia & Pacific	
57%	61%	56%	67%	89%	82%

Goal 5
Improving Maternal Health

Worldwide, more than 50 million women suffer from serious pregnancy-related illness and disability. And every year more than 500,000 women die from complications of pregnancy and childbirth. What makes maternal mortality such a compelling problem is that it strikes young women experiencing a natural function of life. They die because they are poor, malnourished, or weakened by disease, and exposed to multiple pregnancies. And they die because they lack access to trained health care workers and modern medical facilities.

Death in childbirth is a rare event in rich countries, where there are typically fewer than 15 maternal deaths for every 100,000 live births. But in the poorest countries of Africa and Asia the rate may be 100 times higher. And because women in poor countries have more children, their lifetime risk of maternal death may be more than 200 times greater than that for women in rich countries. There is some evidence of progress. More women have access to reproductive health services, and in many places births are more likely to be attended by trained health staff. But few countries are now on track to achieve this Millennium Development Goal.

A woman's risk of death from pregnancy
Sub-Saharan Africa:
1 in 16
North America:
1 in 3,500

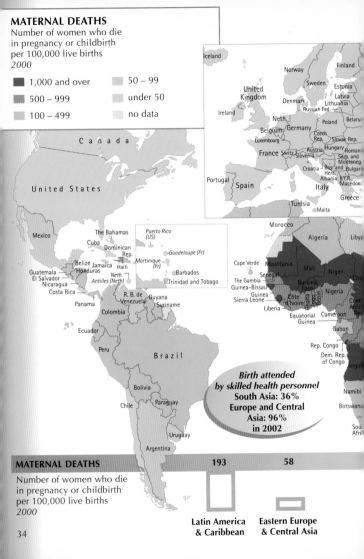

MATERNAL DEATHS

Number of women who die
in pregnancy or childbirth
per 100,000 live births
2000

- 1,000 and over
- 500 – 999
- 100 – 499
- 50 – 99
- under 50
- no data

*Birth attended
by skilled health personnel*
**South Asia: 36%
Europe and Central
Asia: 96%
in 2002**

MATERNAL DEATHS

Number of women who die
in pregnancy or childbirth
per 100,000 live births
2000

193	58
Latin America & Caribbean	**Eastern Europe & Central Asia**

Maternal Mortality

Ninety-nine percent of maternal deaths occur in developing countries, with more than half occurring in Africa. In many poor African countries, one mother dies for every 100 children born.

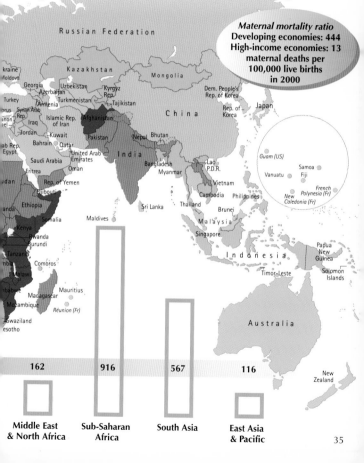

Maternal mortality ratio
Developing economies: 444
High-income economies: 13
maternal deaths per
100,000 live births
in 2000

Middle East & North Africa	Sub-Saharan Africa	South Asia	East Asia & Pacific
162	916	567	116

Combating Disease

Epidemic diseases exact a huge toll in human suffering and lost opportunities for development. Poverty, armed conflict, and natural disasters contribute to the spread of disease and are made worse by it. HIV/AIDS, tuberculosis, and malaria are among the world's biggest killers. Effective prevention and treatment programs will save lives, reduce poverty, and help economies develop.

In Africa the spread of HIV/AIDS has reversed decades of improvements in life expectancy and left millions of children orphaned. It is draining the supply of teachers and eroding the quality of education.

There are 300–500 million cases of malaria each year, leading to more than 1 million deaths. Nearly all the cases (almost 90 percent) occur in Sub-Saharan Africa, and most deaths from malaria are among children younger than five years old.

Tuberculosis kills some 2 million people a year, most of them 15–45 years old. The disease is spreading more rapidly because of the emergence of drug-resistant strains of tuberculosis; the spread of HIV/AIDS, which reduces resistance; and the growing number of refugees and displaced people.

Economic impact
Malaria is estimated to slow economic growth in Sub-Saharan Africa by 1.3 percentage points a year.

PREVALENCE OF HIV

Prevalence of HIV in adult population
ages 15–49 years
2003

- 20.0% and over
- 10.0% – 19.9%
- 1.0% – 9.9%
- 0.5% – 0.9%
- under 0.5%
- no data

PREVALENCE OF HIV

Prevalence of HIV in
people age 15–49 years
2003

2.1%

Low-income
economies

38

AIDS is the leading cause of death in Sub-Saharan Africa and the fourth-largest killer worldwide. Almost 40 million people are living with HIV/AIDS, and the disease poses an unprecedented public health, economic, and social challenge.

Russian Federation

New infections worldwide
14,000 people each day,
over 50% under age 25

Ukraine
Moldova
Kazakhstan
Mongolia
Georgia
Uzbekistan
Kyrgyz Rep.
Azerbaijan
Armenia
Turkmenistan
Tajikistan
China
Rep. of Korea
Japan
Syrian Arab Rep.
Lebanon
Israel
Iraq
Islamic Rep. of Iran
Jordan
Pakistan
Nepal
Arab Rep. of Egypt
Bahrain
India
Eritrea
Oman
Rep. of Yemen
Myanmar
Lao P.D.R.
Vietnam
Sudan
Djibouti
Cambodia
Philippines
Uganda
Ethiopia
Sri Lanka
Thailand
Brunei
Fiji
Kenya
Malaysia
Singapore
Rwanda
Burundi
Tanzania
Indonesia
Papua New Guinea
Zambia
Malawi
Zimbabwe
Madagascar
Mozambique

Sub-Saharan Africa
7% of adults
are living with HIV

Australia

Swaziland
Lesotho

0.7%

0.4%

Middle-income economies

High-income economies

New Zealand

39

TUBERCULOSIS

Incidence of disease
per 100,000 people
2003

- 500 and over
- 250 – 499
- 100 – 249
- 50 – 99
- under 50
- no data

On the increase
**The number of
new TB cases is
increasing by about
1% each year**

1990
2003

TUBERCULOSIS TRENDS

Incidence of disease
per 100,000 people
1990–2003

Latin America & Caribbean	Eastern Europe & Central Asia	Middle East & North Africa
102 66	50 82	61 55

40

Tuberculosis

Tuberculosis kills around 1.7 million people a year. It is the main cause of death from a single infectious agent among adults in developing countries. The rate of new cases is highest in Africa, where TB attacks those infected with HIV.

New cases each year 8 million worldwide; 3 million of them in South and East Asia

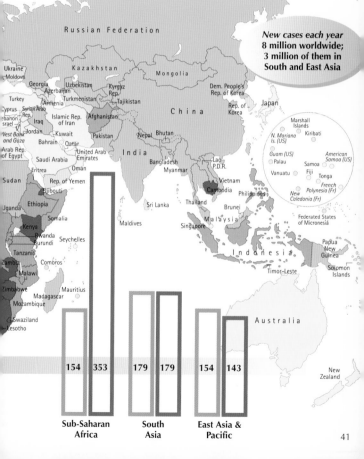

Sub-Saharan Africa		South Asia		East Asia & Pacific	
154	353	179	179	154	143

Ensuring Environmental Sustainability

Sustainable development can be ensured only by protecting the environment and using its resources wisely. Poor people, often dependent on natural resources for their livelihood, are the most affected by environmental degradation and natural disasters, the effects of which are worsened by environmental mismanagement.

Although many countries have adopted principles of sustainable development and agreed to international accords on protecting the environment, land is still being degraded. Forests are being lost and fisheries overused, plant and animal species are becoming extinct, and carbon emissions are leading to climate change.

Rich and poor countries alike have a stake in using environmental resources wisely. Good policies and economic growth, which improve people's lives, can improve the environment.

The MDGs also call for improvements in the built environment. The world may achieve the target for access to water services, but improvement in basic sanitation services has been slow, and slums are growing as more people move into urban areas.

Improved water supplies in developing countries
Percentage of people with access:
1990: 72%
2002: 79%

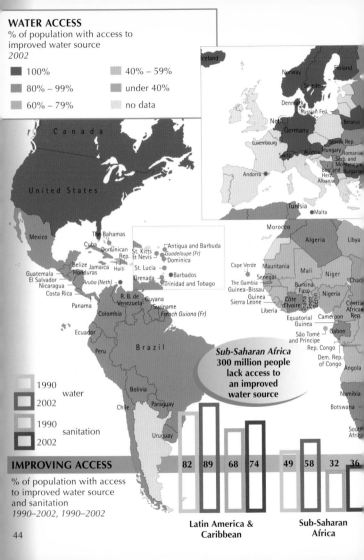

WATER ACCESS
% of population with access to improved water source
2002

- ■ 100%
- ■ 80% – 99%
- ■ 60% – 79%
- ■ 40% – 59%
- ■ under 40%
- □ no data

Canada

United States

Mexico

The Bahamas
Cuba
Dominican Rep.
St. Kitts & Nevis
Guadeloupe (Fr)
Antigua and Barbuda
Dominica
St. Lucia
Barbados
Trinidad and Tobago
Grenada
Belize
Jamaica
Honduras
Haiti
Aruba (Neth)
Guatemala
El Salvador
Nicaragua
Costa Rica
Panama
Colombia
R. B. de Venezuela
Guyana
Suriname
French Guiana (Fr)
Ecuador
Peru
Brazil
Bolivia
Chile
Paraguay
Uruguay

Iceland
Norway
Finland
Sweden
Denmark
Russian Fed.
Belarus
Neth.
Germany
Luxembourg
Switz.
Austria
Slovak Rep.
Hungary
Romania
Serb. and Montenegro
Bos. and Herz.
Bulgaria
Andorra
Albania
Tunisia
Malta

Morocco
Algeria
Libya
Cape Verde
Mauritania
Mali
Niger
Chad
Senegal
Burkina Faso
Nigeria
The Gambia
Guinea-Bissau
Guinea
Sierra Leone
Côte d'Ivoire
Ghana
Togo
Benin
Liberia
Central African Rep.
Equatorial Guinea
Cameroon
São Tomé and Principe
Gabon
Rep. Congo
Dem. Rep. of Congo
Angola
Namibia
Botswana
South Africa

Sub-Saharan Africa
300 million people lack access to an improved water source

- □ 1990 / water
- ■ 2002
- □ 1990 / sanitation
- ■ 2002

IMPROVING ACCESS
% of population with access to improved water source and sanitation
1990–2002, 1990–2002

	Latin America & Caribbean				Sub-Saharan Africa		
	82	89	68	74	49	58	32	36

44

Water and Sanitation

Access to safe drinking water and basic sanitation has increased, but in 2002 1.1 billion people still lacked access to a reliable source of water that was reasonably protected from contamination, and 2.4 billion people were still in need of improved sanitation services.

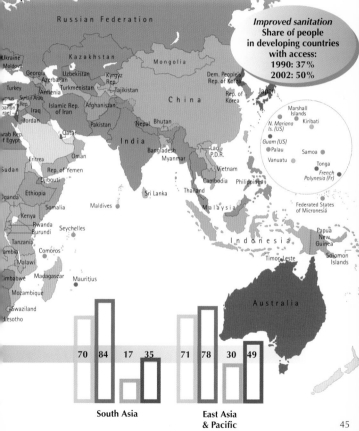

Improved sanitation
Share of people in developing countries with access:
1990: 37%
2002: 50%

	South Asia				East Asia & Pacific		
	70	84	17	35	71	78	30	49

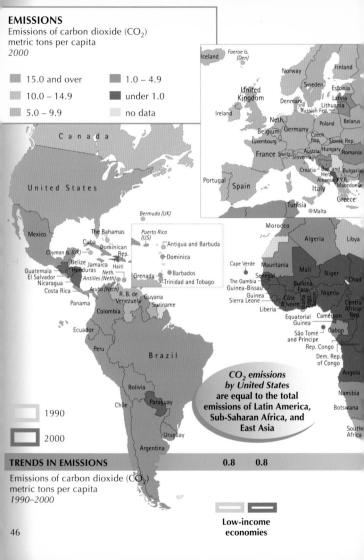

EMISSIONS

Emissions of carbon dioxide (CO$_2$)
metric tons per capita
2000

- 15.0 and over
- 10.0 – 14.9
- 5.0 – 9.9
- 1.0 – 4.9
- under 1.0
- no data

*CO$_2$ emissions
by United States
are equal to the total
emissions of Latin America,
Sub-Saharan Africa, and
East Asia*

1990

2000

TRENDS IN EMISSIONS

0.8   0.8

Emissions of carbon dioxide (CO$_2$)
metric tons per capita
1990–2000

Low-income
economies

Carbon Dioxide

Emissions of carbon dioxide (CO_2), a greenhouse gas that contributes to global climate change, have increased in most developing regions. But high-income economies remain the largest emitters of carbon dioxide.

High-income countries account for half the world's CO_2 emissions

3.6	3.2	11.8	12.4

Middle-income economies   High-income economies

Goal 8

Developing a Global Partnership

What will it take to achieve the Millennium Development Goals? A lot. Economies need to grow to provide jobs and incomes for poor people. Health and education systems must deliver services to everyone: men and women, rich and poor. Infrastructure has to work and be accessible to all. And policies need to empower people to participate in the development process. While success depends on the actions of developing countries, which must direct their own development, there is also much that rich countries must do to help. This is what Goal 8 is for – it complements the first seven.

Goal 8 calls for an open, rule-based trading and financial system, more generous aid to countries committed to poverty reduction, and relief for the debt problems of developing countries. It draws attention to the problems of the least developed countries and of landlocked countries and small-island developing states, which have greater difficulty competing in the global economy. It also calls for cooperation with the private sector to address youth unemployment, ensure access to affordable, essential drugs, and make available the benefits of new information and communication technologies.

> Official development assistance to developing countries reached $78.6 billion in 2004, its highest level ever. This represents a 4.6% increase over 2003.

49

GIVING AND RECEIVING

Net value of aid and development assistance
US$ per capita *2003*

Aid received:
- over $100
- $51 – $100
- $50 and under

Aid donated:
- over $100
- $51 – $100
- $50 and under
- no data or no aid

Finland
Norway
Sweden
Estonia
United Kingdom
Denmark
Latvia
Lithuania
Ireland
Russian Fed.
Neth.
Poland
Belaru
Belgium
Germany
Czech Rep.
Slovak Rep.
France
Switz.
Austria
Hungary
Roman
Slovenia
Serb. and
Croatia
Bos. and
Monteneg.
Herz.
Bulgar
Portugal
Spain
Albania
F.Y.R.
Macedor
Italy
Greece
Tunisia

Canada

United States

Mexico
Cuba
Dominican Rep.
Jamaica Haiti
Guatemala Honduras
El Salvador
Nicaragua
Costa Rica
Panama
R. B. de
Venezuela
Trinidad and Tobago
Colombia
Ecuador
Peru
Brazil
Bolivia
Paraguay
Chile
Uruguay
Argentina

Morocco
Algeria
Liby
Mauritania
Mali
Niger
Ch
Senegal
Burkina
The Gambia
Faso
Nigeria
Guinea-Bissau
Guinea
Côte
Ghana
Sierra Leone
d'Ivoire
Liberia
Cen
Afric
Re
Cameroon
Gabon
Rep. Congo
Dem. Rep.
of Congo
Ango
Namib
Botswana
So
Afr

***Donations
as percentage of GNI***
Average: 0.25%
UN target: 0.7%

DONOR EFFORT	Norway	Netherlands	Sweden	Belgium
	0.92	0.80	0.79	0.60

Net ODA as a % of GNI
2003

Official development assistance (ODA) is provided by the richest countries to the poorest. Through much of the 1990s ODA levels fell. Since 2002 donors have pledged to increase aid by $20 billion a year in 2006 and to provide more than $100 billion a year by 2010. But new commitments will meet only a fraction of the need.

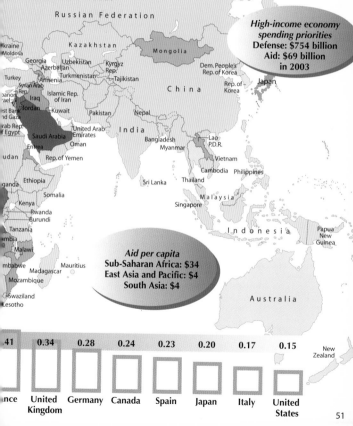

Russian Federation

kraine
Moldova
Georgia
Azerbaijan
Turkey
Syrian Arab Rep.
banon
ael Iraq
st Bank Jordan
nd Gaza
rab Rep.
f Egypt
Saudi Arabia
udan
Rep. of Yemen

Kazakhstan

Uzbekistan
Turkmenistan
Armenia
Islamic Rep.
of Iran
Kuwait
United Arab
Emirates
Oman

Kyrgyz
Rep.
Tajikistan

Mongolia

Dem. People's
Rep. of Korea

China

Pakistan
Nepal

India

Bangladesh

Rep. of
Korea

Japan

Lao
P.D.R.
Myanmar

Sri Lanka

Vietnam

Cambodia Philippines

Thailand

*High-income economy
spending priorities*
**Defense: $754 billion
Aid: $69 billion
in 2003**

ganda
Ethiopia
Somalia
Kenya
Rwanda
Burundi
Tanzania
mbia
Malawi
mbabwe
Mozambique
Swaziland
Lesotho

Madagascar

Mauritius

Malaysia

Singapore

Indonesia

Papua
New
Guinea

Aid per capita
**Sub-Saharan Africa: $34
East Asia and Pacific: $4
South Asia: $4**

Australia

.41	0.34	0.28	0.24	0.23	0.20	0.17	0.15	
nce	United Kingdom	Germany	Canada	Spain	Japan	Italy	United States	New Zealand

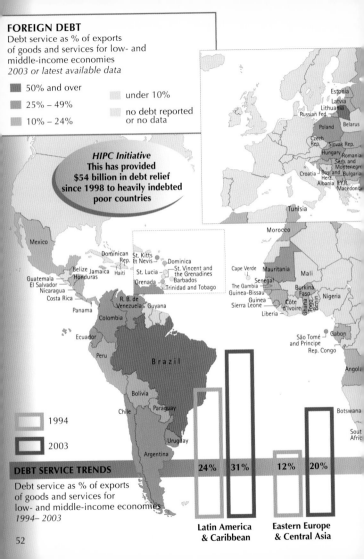

FOREIGN DEBT
Debt service as % of exports
of goods and services for low- and
middle-income economies
2003 or latest available data

- 50% and over
- 25% – 49%
- 10% – 24%
- under 10%
- no debt reported or no data

HIPC Initiative
**This has provided
$54 billion in debt relief
since 1998 to heavily indebted
poor countries**

1994
2003

DEBT SERVICE TRENDS

Debt service as % of exports
of goods and services for
low- and middle-income economies
1994– 2003

24%   31%   12%   20%

**Latin America
& Caribbean**

**Eastern Europe
& Central Asia**

52

Debt service measures the relative burden on developing countries of their external debt. In many countries, export earnings, by which debtor countries acquire the currencies to pay their creditors, have been rising, while debt service has grown more slowly, reducing their debt burdens.

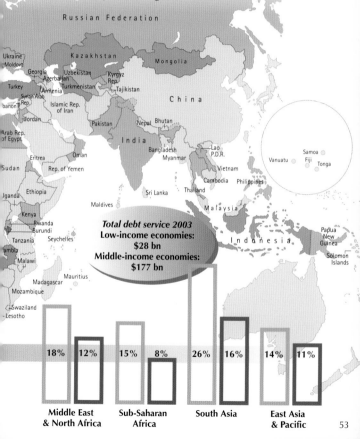

Total debt service 2003
Low-income economies:
$28 bn
Middle-income economies:
$177 bn

Middle East & North Africa		Sub-Saharan Africa		South Asia		East Asia & Pacific	
18%	12%	15%	8%	26%	16%	14%	11%

Countries	COUNTRY PROFILE		POVERTY AND HUNGER	
	Population 2003 millions	GNI per capita Atlas method 2003 US$	Under $1 per day % of pop. 1995–2003	Malnourished children under 5 years as % of total 1995–2003
Afghanistan	–	–	–	49
Albania	3.2	1,740	<2	14
Algeria	31.8	1,930	<2	6
Angola	13.5	740	–	31
Argentina	36.8	3,810	3	5
Armenia	3.1	950	13	3
Australia	19.9	21,950	–	0
Austria	8.1	26,810	–	–
Azerbaijan	8.2	820	4	7
Bangladesh	138.1	400	36	52
Belarus	9.9	1,600	<2	–
Belgium	10.4	25,760	–	–
Benin	6.7	440	–	23
Bolivia	8.8	900	14	8
Bosnia and Herzegovina	4.1	1,530	–	4
Botswana	1.7	3,530	–	13
Brazil	176.6	2,720	8	6
Bulgaria	7.8	2,130	5	–
Burkina Faso	12.1	300	45	38
Burundi	7.2	90	55	45
Cambodia	13.4	300	34	45
Cameroon	16.1	630	17	22
Canada	31.6	24,470	–	–
Central African Republic	3.9	260	–	23
Chad	8.6	240	–	28
Chile	15.8	4,360	<2	1
China	1,288.4	1,100	17	10
Hong Kong, China	6.8	25,860	–	–
Colombia	44.6	1,810	8	7
Congo, Dem. Rep.	53.2	100	–	31
Congo, Rep.	3.8	650	–	–
Costa Rica	4.0	4,300	<2	5
Côte d'Ivoire	16.8	660	11	21
Croatia	4.4	5,370	<2	1

PRIMARY EDUCATION	GENDER EQUALITY	CHILD MORTALITY	MATERNAL HEALTH	DISEASE	ENVIRONMENT	GLOBAL PARTNERSHIP
% of children completing 2000–2003	Gender parity index 1998–2002	Under-five mortality rate per 1,000 2002–2003	Maternal mortality per 100,000 live births 2000	HIV prevalence in adult pop. ages 15–49 2003	Access to improved water source % of pop. 2002	Debt service as % of goods and services 2003 or latest
–	52	–	1,900	–	13	–
101	102	21	55	–	97	3
96	99	41	140	0.1	87	–
–	–	260	1,700	3.9	50	15
103	103	20	82	0.7	–	38
110	101	33	55	0.1	92	9
–	99	6	8	0.1	100	–
101	97	6	4	0.3	100	–
106	97	91	94	<0.1	77	8
73	107	69	380	–	75	6
99	102	17	35	–	100	2
–	107	5	10	0.2	–	–
51	66	154	850	1.9	68	–
101	98	66	420	0.1	85	21
–	–	17	31	<0.1	98	6
91	102	112	100	37.3	95	1
112	103	35	260	0.7	89	64
97	98	17	32	0.1	100	11
29	72	207	1,000	1.8	51	11
31	79	190	1,000	6.0	79	66
81	85	140	450	2.6	34	1
70	85	166	730	6.9	63	–
–	100	7	6	0.3	100	–
–	–	180	1,100	13.5	75	–
25	59	200	1,100	4.8	34	–
104	100	9	31	0.3	95	31
98	97	37	56	0.1	77	7
101	100	–	–	0.1	–	–
88	104	21	130	0.7	92	44
–	–	205	990	4.2	46	–
59	87	108	510	4.9	46	4
94	101	10	43	0.6	97	10
51	69	192	690	7.0	84	9
96	101	7	8	<0.1	–	21

Countries	COUNTRY PROFILE		POVERTY AND HUNGER	
	Population *2003* millions	GNI per capita Atlas method *2003* US$	Under $1 per day % of pop. *1995–2003*	Malnourished children under 5 years as % of total *1995–2003*
Cuba	11.3	–	–	4
Czech Republic	10.2	7,150	<2	–
Denmark	5.4	33,570	–	–
Dominican Republic	8.7	2,130	<2	5
Ecuador	13.0	1,830	18	14
Egypt, Arab Rep.	67.6	1,390	3	9
El Salvador	6.5	2,340	31	10
Eritrea	4.4	190	–	40
Estonia	1.4	5,380	<2	–
Ethiopia	68.6	90	23	47
Finland	5.2	27,060	–	–
France	59.8	24,730	–	–
Gabon	1.3	3,340	–	12
Gambia, The	1.4	270	–	17
Georgia	5.1	770	3	3
Germany	82.5	25,270	–	–
Ghana	20.7	320	45	22
Greece	11.0	13,230	–	–
Guatemala	12.3	1,910	16	23
Guinea	7.9	430	–	23
Guinea-Bissau	1.5	140	–	25
Haiti	8.4	400	–	17
Honduras	7.0	970	21	17
Hungary	10.1	6,350	<2	–
India	1,064.4	540	35	47
Indonesia	214.7	810	8	27
Iran, Islamic Rep.	66.4	2,010	<2	11
Iraq	24.7	–	–	16
Ireland	4.0	27,010	–	–
Israel	6.7	16,240	–	–
Italy	57.6	21,570	–	–
Jamaica	2.6	2,980	<2	4
Japan	127.6	34,180	–	–
Jordan	5.3	1,850	<2	4

PRIMARY EDUCATION	GENDER EQUALITY	CHILD MORTALITY	MATERNAL HEALTH	DISEASE	ENVIRONMENT	GLOBAL PARTNERSHIP
% of children completing 2000–2003	Gender parity index 1998–2002	Under-five mortality rate per 1,000 2002–2003	Maternal mortality per 100,000 live births 2000	HIV prevalence in adult pop. ages 15–49 2003	Access to improved water source % of pop. 2002	Debt service as % of goods and services 2003 or latest
94	97	8	33	0.1	91	–
106	101	5	9	0.1	–	9
107	103	6	5	0.2	100	–
93	108	35	150	1.7	93	8
100	100	27	130	0.3	86	28
91	93	39	84	<0.1	98	12
89	96	36	150	0.7	82	9
40	76	85	630	2.7	57	14
104	99	9	63	1.1	–	17
39	69	169	850	4.4	22	7
101	106	4	6	0.1	100	–
–	100	6	17	0.4	–	–
74	96	91	420	8.1	87	–
68	90	123	540	1.2	82	–
82	100	45	32	0.1	76	12
101	99	5	8	0.1	100	–
62	91	95	540	3.1	79	15
–	101	5	9	0.2	–	–
66	93	47	240	1.1	95	7
41	69	160	740	3.2	51	15
–	65	204	1,100	–	59	16
–	–	118	680	5.6	71	4
79		41	110	1.8	90	12
102	100	7	16	0.1	99	29
81	80	87	540	0.9	86	18
95	98	41	230	0.1	78	26
107	96	39	76	0.1	93	4
–	80	125	250	<0.1	81	–
–	104	7	5	0.1	–	–
–	99	6	17	0.1	100	–
101	97	6	5	0.5	–	–
85	101	20	87	1.2	93	16
–	100	5	10	<0.1	100	–
98	101	28	41	<0.1	91	16

Countries	COUNTRY PROFILE		POVERTY AND HUNGER	
	Population 2003 millions	GNI per capita Atlas method 2003 US$	Under $1 per day % of pop. 1995-2003	Malnourished children under 5 years as % of total 1995-2003
Kazakhstan	14.9	1,780	<2	4
Kenya	31.9	400	23	20
Korea, Dem. Rep.	22.6	–	–	28
Korea, Rep.	47.9	12,030	<2	–
Kuwait	2.4	17,960	–	2
Kyrgyz Republic	5.1	340	<2	6
Lao PDR	5.7	340	26	40
Latvia	2.3	4,400	<2	–
Lebanon	4.5	4,040	–	3
Lesotho	1.8	610	36	18
Liberia	3.4	110	–	27
Libya	5.6	–	–	5
Lithuania	3.5	4,500	<2	–
Macedonia, FYR	2.0	1,980	<2	6
Madagascar	16.9	290	61	33
Malawi	11.0	160	42	25
Malaysia	24.8	3,880	<2	19
Mali	11.7	290	–	33
Mauritania	2.8	400	26	32
Mauritius	1.2	4,100	–	15
Mexico	102.3	6,230	10	8
Moldova	4.2	590	22	–
Mongolia	2.5	480	27	13
Morocco	30.1	1,310	<2	9
Mozambique	18.8	210	38	26
Myanmar	49.4	–	–	28
Namibia	2.0	1,930	–	24
Nepal	24.7	240	39	48
Netherlands	16.2	26,230	–	–
New Zealand	4.0	15,530	–	–
Nicaragua	5.5	740	45	10
Niger	11.8	200	61	40
Nigeria	136.5	350	70	29
Norway	4.6	43,400	–	–

PRIMARY EDUCATION	GENDER EQUALITY	CHILD MORTALITY	MATERNAL HEALTH	DISEASE	ENVIRONMENT	GLOBAL PARTNERSHIP
% of children completing 2000–2003	Gender parity index 1998–2002	Under-five mortality rate per 1,000 2002–2003	Maternal mortality per 100,000 live births 2000	HIV prevalence in adult pop. ages 15–49 2003	Access to improved water source % of pop. 2002	Debt service as % of goods and services 2003 or latest
110	100	73	210	0.2	86	35
73	94	123	1,000	6.7	62	16
–	–	55	67	–	100	–
97	100	5	20	<0.1	92	–
96	104	9	5	–	–	–
93	100	68	110	0.1	76	16
74	83	91	650	0.1	43	10
101	100	12	42	0.6	–	18
68	102	31	150	0.1	100	66
67	105	110	550	28.9	76	9
–	72	235	760	5.9	62	0
–	103	16	97	0.3	72	–
102	99	11	13	0.1	–	68
100	99	11	23	<0.1	–	13
47	97	126	550	1.7	45	6
71	92	178	1,800	14.2	67	8
92	104	7	41	0.4	95	8
40	71	220	1,200	1.9	48	–
43	94	107	1,000	0.6	56	–
105	101	18	24	–	100	7
99	102	28	83	0.3	91	21
83	102	32	36	0.2	92	10
108	110	68	110	<0.1	62	32
75	88	39	220	0.1	80	24
52	79	147	1,000	12.2	42	7
73	99	107	360	1.2	80	4
92	104	65	300	21.3	80	–
78	83	82	740	0.5	84	6
98	98	6	16	0.2	100	–
–	103	6	7	0.1	–	–
75	104	38	230	0.2	81	12
26	69	262	1,600	1.2	46	–
82	–	198	800	5.4	60	–
–	101	5	16	0.1	100	–

Countries	COUNTRY PROFILE		POVERTY AND HUNGER	
	Population 2003 millions	GNI per capita Atlas method 2003 US$	Under $1 per day % of pop. 1995–2003	Malnourished children under 5 years as % of total 1995–2003
Oman	2.6	–	–	18
Pakistan	148.4	520	13	35
Panama	3.0	4,060	7	8
Papua New Guinea	5.5	500	–	–
Paraguay	5.6	1,110	16	–
Peru	27.1	2,140	18	7
Philippines	81.5	1,080	15	32
Poland	38.2	5,280	<2	–
Portugal	10.4	11,800	–	–
Puerto Rico	3.9	–	–	–
Romania	21.7	2,260	<2	3
Russian Federation	143.4	2,610	<2	6
Rwanda	8.4	220	52	24
Saudi Arabia	22.5	9,240	–	–
Senegal	10.2	540	22	23
Serbia and Montenegro	8.1	1,910	–	2
Sierra Leone	5.3	150	–	27
Singapore	4.3	21,230	–	3
Slovak Republic	5.4	4,940	<2	–
Slovenia	2.0	11,920	<2	–
Somalia	9.6	–	–	26
South Africa	45.8	2,750	11	12
Spain	41.1	17,040	–	–
Sri Lanka	19.2	930	8	33
Sudan	33.5	460	–	41
Swaziland	1.1	1,350	–	10
Sweden	9.0	28,910	–	–
Switzerland	7.4	40,680	–	–
Syrian Arab Republic	17.4	1,160	–	7
Tajikistan	6.3	210	7	–
Tanzania	35.9	300	–	29
Thailand	62.0	2,190	<2	18
Togo	4.9	310	–	25
Trinidad and Tobago	1.3	7,790	–	6

PRIMARY EDUCATION	GENDER EQUALITY	CHILD MORTALITY	MATERNAL HEALTH	DISEASE	ENVIRONMENT	GLOBAL PARTNERSHIP
% of children completing *2000–2003*	Gender parity index *1998–2002*	Under-five mortality rate per 1,000 *2002–2003*	Maternal mortality per 100,000 live births *2000*	HIV prevalence in adult pop. ages 15–49 *2003*	Access to improved water source % of pop. *2002*	Debt service as % of goods and services *2003 or latest*
73	97	12	87	0.1	79	10
–	71	98	500	0.1	90	16
98	100	24	160	0.9	91	11
53	88	93	300	0.6	39	12
93	98	29	170	0.5	83	10
102	97	34	410	0.5	81	22
95	102	36	200	<0.1	85	22
98	98	7	13	0.1	–	25
–	102	5	5	0.4	–	–
–	–	–	25	–	–	–
89	100	20	49	<0.1	57	17
93	100	21	67	1.1	96	12
37	95	203	1,400	5.1	73	14
61	93	26	23	–	–	–
48	87	137	690	0.8	72	10
96	101	14	11	0.2	93	14
56	70	284	2,000	–	57	12
–	–	5	30	0.2	–	–
99	101	8	3	<0.1	100	13
95	100	4	17	<0.1	–	–
–	–	225	1,100	–	29	–
99	100	66	230	15.6	87	9
–	103	4	4	0.7	–	–
–	103	15	92	<0.1	78	7
49	86	93	590	2.3	69	1
75	94	153	370	38.8	52	2
101	112	4	2	0.1	100	–
99	96	6	7	0.4	100	–
88	93	18	160	<0.1	79	4
100	88	95	100	<0.1	58	9
58	99	165	1,500	8.8	73	5
86	95	26	44	1.5	85	16
78	69	140	570	4.1	51	2
91	102	20	160	3.2	91	4

Countries	COUNTRY PROFILE		POVERTY AND HUNGER	
	Population 2003 millions	GNI per capita Atlas method 2003 US$	Under $1 per day % of pop. 1995–2003	Malnourished children under 5 years as % of total 1995–2003
Tunisia	9.9	2,240	<2	4
Turkey	70.7	2,800	<2	8
Turkmenistan	4.9	1,120	12	12
Uganda	25.3	250	85	23
Ukraine	48.4	970	3	3
United Arab Emirates	4.0	–	–	7
United Kingdom	59.3	28,320	–	–
United States	290.8	37,870	–	–
Uruguay	3.4	3,820	<2	–
Uzbekistan	25.6	420	17	8
Venezuela, RB	25.7	3,490	14	4
Vietnam	81.3	480	<2	34
West Bank and Gaza	3.4	1,110	–	4
Yemen, Rep.	19.2	520	16	46
Zambia	10.4	380	64	28
Zimbabwe	13.1	–	56	13
World	6,272.5	5,510	–	–
Low income	2,311.9	440	–	–
Middle income	2,988.6	1,930	–	–
Lower middle income	2,655.5	1,490	–	–
Upper middle income	333.1	5,440	–	–
Low & middle income	5,300.5	1,280	21	–
East Asia & Pacific	1,854.6	1,070	15	16
Europe & Central Asia	472.2	2,580	4	7
Latin America & Caribbean	532.7	3,280	10	8
Middle East & North Africa	311.6	2,390	<2	8
South Asia	1,424.7	510	31	45
Sub-Saharan Africa	704.5	500	46	30
High income	972.1	28,600	–	–

PRIMARY EDUCATION	GENDER EQUALITY	CHILD MORTALITY	MATERNAL HEALTH	DISEASE	ENVIRONMENT	GLOBAL PARTNERSHIP
% of children completing 2000–2003	Gender parity index 1998–2002	Under-five mortality rate per 1,000 2002–2003	Maternal mortality per 100,000 live births 2000	HIV prevalence in adult pop. ages 15–49 2003	Access to improved water source % of pop. 2002	Debt service as % of goods and services 2003 or latest
101	100	24	120	<0.1	82	13
95	85	39	70	–	93	38
–	–	102	31	<0.1	71	–
63	96	140	880	4.1	56	7
59	99	20	35	1.4	98	13
71	100	8	54	–	–	–
–	116	7	13	0.2	–	–
–	100	8	17	0.6	100	–
92	105	14	27	0.3	98	26
103	98	69	24	0.1	89	21
90	104	21	96	0.7	83	30
95	93	23	130	0.4	73	3
106	–	–	–	–	–	–
66	61	113	570	0.1	69	3
69	91	182	750	15.6	55	28
81	95	126	1,100	24.6	83	–
–	93	86	407	1.1	82	–
71	84	123	689	2.1	75	12
95	98	37	115	0.7	83	18
95	97	39	121	0.7	82	18
93	102	22	67	0.6	–	18
84	91	87	444	1.2	79	17
97	97	41	116	0.2	78	11
90	97	36	58	0.7	91	20
96	102	33	193	0.7	89	31
84	91	53	162	0.1	88	12
80	82	92	567	0.8	84	16
59	84	171	916	7.2	58	8
–	101	7	13	0.4	99	–

Index

Definitions, Notes, and Sources

Definitions

Aid: refers to grants and disbursements of concessional loans (net of repayments) provided for development purposes by official agencies of members of the OECD's Development Committee, by some other countries, and by multilateral institutions such as the World Bank. Military assistance is not included in aid.

AIDS: acquired immune deficiency syndrome

Carbon dioxide emissions: emissions stemming from the burning of fossil fuels and the manufacture of cement. They include carbon dioxide produced during consumption of solid, liquid, and gas fuels and gas flaring. (Source: Carbon Dioxide Information Analysis Center)

Child malnutrition: the percentage of children whose weight for age is more than two standard deviations below the median for the international reference population ages 0-59 months. (Source: WHO)

CO_2: carbon dioxide

Debt service as a share of exports: the ratio of public and publicly guaranteed debt service (after debt relief) to the exports of goods and services and net income from abroad. (Source: IMF and World Bank)

Extreme poverty: the percentage of the population living on less than $1.08 a day at 1993 international prices. (Source: World Bank)

Gender parity index in primary and secondary: the ratio of girls' to boys' gross enrollment rates in primary and secondary school. A value less than 100 indicates that girls are under represented in primary and secondary school. (Source: UNESCO)

Gross Domestic Product (GDP): the sum of gross value added by all resident producers in the economy plus any product taxes (less subsidies) not included in the value of the products. It is calculated using purchaser prices and without deductions for the depreciation of fabricated assets or for the depletion and degradation of natural resources.

Gross National Income (GNI): gross national income (formerly called gross national product or GNP) is the sum of gross value added by all resident producers plus any taxes (less subsidies) that are not included in the valuation of output plus net receipts of primary income (employee compensation and property income) from nonresident sources. GNI per capita is in current US dollars converted using the World Bank Atlas method.

Heavily Indebted Poor Countries (HIPC) Initiative: an initiative by official creditors designed to help the poorest, most heavily indebted countries escape from unsustainable debt.

HIV: human immunodeficiency virus

HIV, prevalence of: refers to the percentage of people age 15-49 who are infected with HIV. (Source: UNAIDS and WHO)

Immunization, measles: the percentage of children ages 12–23 months at the time of the survey who received a dose of measles vaccine by the age of 12 months, or at any time before the interview date. A child is considered adequately immunized against measles after receiving one dose of vaccine. (Source: WHO and UNICEF)

Maternal mortality ratio: the number of women who die from pregnancy-related causes during pregnancy and childbirth, per 100,000 live births. Data are based on modeled estimates. (Source: WHO and UNICEF)

Millennium Development Goals (MDGs): eight goals for sustainable development contained in the Millennium Declaration adopted unanimously by the 189 members of the United Nations in September 2000. (*See inside front cover for a list of the MDGs.*)

Mortality rate, under-five: the probability that a newborn baby will die before reaching the age of five, if subject to current age-specific mortality rates. (Source: UN, UNICEF)

Net aid per capita: receipts refer to official development assistance, and official aid received from members of the OECD Development Assistance Committee and other official donors net of repayments and aid donated. Countries whose repayments and donations exceed their receipts are shown as net aid donors. (Source: OECD DAC)

Related World Bank Titles

World Development Indicators 2005
Consult over 800 indicators for 152 economies
and 14 country groups in more than 80 tables.
Provides a current overview of the most recent
data available as well as important regional data
and income group analysis in six thematic
chapters. Also available on CD-ROM.
ISBN: 0-8213-6071-X

World Development Indicators Online
The premier data source on the global economy,
WDI Online contains statistical data for over 575
development indicators and time series data from
1960-2002 for over 220 countries and country
groups. Updated periodically with annual data
loaded in May.
www.worldbank.org/online

World Bank Atlas, 36th edition
With its easy-to-read and colorful world maps,
tables, and graphs, the *World Bank Atlas* vividly
illustrates the key development challenges in the
world today.
ISBN: 0-8213-5732-8

Little Data Book 2005
A pocket-sized ready reference on key
development data for 208 countries.
ISBN: 0-8213-6075-2

**To order, phone 1-800-645-7247 or 703-661-
1580 or go to www.worldbank.org/publications.**

Prices and credit terms vary from country to
country. Please consult your local distributor or
bookseller before placing an order.